The Heart of the Nation

31 Day Devotional Guide
for the Journey Home

The Heart of the Nation

31 Day Devotional Guide
for the Journey Home

by
Mark A. Smith

Chazown Publishing Company

South Bend, Indiana

For more information on the ideas and concepts presented in this material, the author recommends reading the bible and diligently praying for God's understanding and knowledge (Proverbs 2:1-5).

Additional copies of this book can be obtained from your local book store or by contacting the publisher. For additional copies of the book, a current list of publications, and other information please write:

Chazown Publishing Company
P.O. Box 1223
South Bend, IN 46624
Tel: (219) 679-9218

Promise Keepers® is a registered trademark of that organization. Any reference to them in this book is not to be construed as an endorsement of this book by that organization and is only used as a historical reference.

ISBN 0-9661709-0-3

Acknowledgements

It is difficult to create a list of people to thank and acknowledge. So many people impact a person's life, how can such a list be created? I'm sure such a list cannot be exhaustive, it can only be created with the best of intent. I want to take a moment to acknowledge and thank those that have been of assistance to me in my own journey. While those listed here may have had no direct input into this book, still I have been blessed to have met so many people.

First, I want to thank the Ross family, Terry, Jayne and Carolyn, of the Budget Printing Center in Mishawaka, Indiana. They have always been professional and fair in their dealings with me, their work is impeccable, and they helped me get the word out about my work.

Next I want to thank George Johnson of Johnson Graphics. Not only is he the printer of the first (and hopefully more) printing of this book, but he took time to educate me about our country. George was able to shed more light on the Constitution of the United States in a few hours than all of my educational experiences combined.

I want to thank Jerry Holland, my friend in business, who also encouraged me in this work. And his wife Sally.

I want to thank Frank and Jenny Gordon for not giving up on me. Also to Hap Leman and Ben Hoerr for teaching me the scriptures.

Of course I want to acknowledge my family, my wife and children. This book is in part dedicated to them. Certainly without them my life would be less.

My brother, Larry, and his family, and my sisters, Ruth and Betty, and their families have always been a source of comfort to me. My ability to reach out to them has taught me much about the character of God.

To all the people at the church we attend, the California Road Missionary Church in Elkhart, Indiana, I say thank you for making me and my family feel welcome.

I want to thank my Mom and Dad. I pray that they like this work, and what they see of me from heaven.

And last I want to thank Rev. Wyatt Smith. He was faithful to speak truth, and did not turn away. Without his faithfulness in that moment, I do not wish to contemplate where my family and I would be today. To God be the Glory.

- Mark A. Smith

To Jesus,
to my wife Kim,
to my daughters Jamie and Katie,
to my son Joshua,
and to those who read these pages.

Thank you,
for you have inspired me
and blessed me
beyond human understanding,
and more than anyone deserves.

Mark A. Smith

The Heart of the Nation

31 Day Devotional Guide
for the Journey Home

by
Mark A. Smith

Table Of Contents

Prologue

PROLOGUE

First, I would like to say thank you for honoring me by reading this book. It is offered to do one thing, to magnify and glorify the One true living God. Before you begin, I offer some thoughts regarding the reading of this material.

I have suggested in the second chapter that this book be used as a way of creating a 31 day journey of renewal and revival for yourself, customized to you and God. While I both know and have experienced this to be a great blessing, please do not set this book aside because you cannot make such a commitment now.

If you want to just use it as a book of poetry, so be it. Perhaps you want to skip around, or even mix this "daily devotional" path with something else you are currently doing. That, too, would be just fine. Please do not take these writings or the suggestions I have made as something to "bind" you up or discourage you. God means for you to experience His holiness and the freedom it brings. This is also my great desire for you. Decide what is best for you, and then do it.

Lastly, I would like to say that I am a believer, as I trust you are (or soon will be). I believe God shared this material with me. He is infallible. I am not. As a wise preacher once told me, "If there is anything in what you are reading or hearing that doesn't seem right, just be smart like a cow. Chew the hay and spit out the sticks." I don't think he was telling me that I was not very bright, just that I should ask God to show me what is right. If, as you read this material, there is anything that you feel detracts from Jesus or His teachings, please disregard it. And pray for me as I have and will for you. Thank you and God bless you!

Yours in Jesus,

Mark A. Smith

Please read these scriptures before you begin.

Hosea 10:12   John 3:16

To God be the glory.

NOTES:

NOTES:

NOTES:

How My Journey Began

Chapter 1

How My Journey Began
- Chapter 1 -

On September 16, 1997, at approximately 5:30 am, I began my journey. I did not know at the time that I was starting a journey. In fact, I had seated myself at the computer in my home office to continue working on another book I was writing about manufacturing practices. Reflecting back, I think it was better that I did not know the details of what was to take place. Perhaps I would have chosen not to attempt this undertaking.

It has become my custom to get up early in the morning to take about an hour or so to read the bible and to pray. That Wednesday morning was no different. After my time with God I was to work on a manufacturing book because I am a business consultant. I had recently incorporated my business and wanted to publish my ideas on new approaches to American manufacturing. At 5:30 I was just about three fourths of the way through my time alone with God. I had something in particular on my mind.

At this point I need to pause to fill in some voids. You

need to know a bit about my past and what lead up to that morning. I became a Christian when I was in elementary school. I don't remember the exact date, but I remember the experience quite well. The mother of a neighbor friend talked with me about Jesus. She showed me some bible passages and prayed with me for forgiveness of my sin. A new beginning. Although I have had struggles in my life, I look back to that moment as my true rebirth in Jesus.

I am providing this information not because it fits well into the overall story, but to give testimony that there is One God, that Jesus bled and died for our sins, that He arose on the third day, He sits at the right hand of the Father, awaiting His return, and that everyone who believes on Him shall have everlasting life. Jesus is my Savior because I confessed my sins to Him and He was merciful to forgive me and grant me everlasting life. He is my Friend. If you don't know Him personally, like a best friend, you can. Call on His name and confess your sins. Ask for forgiveness and He will grant *you* everlasting life, too. Anyway, back to the journey.

Sitting at my computer, I reflected. My wife and I recently began attending a church very near our home.

Earlier in the spring the pastor had been giving some announcements about an upcoming event. Stand in the Gap, a Promise Keepers® event, was to happen in October. I was only slightly familiar with the organization. I remembered in my past reading about the sacred assemblies in Israel. My wife and I both agreed that I should attend. On that morning in September, the day was drawing close.

As I thought about the upcoming trip to Washington, D.C., I wondered about the purpose. I knew I wanted to go, felt I should go, but what was I expecting to get out of it? As one who believes that the Holy Spirit is still alive and well on planet earth, what did I think I would experience? I remember feeling that somehow I needed to do something, wanted to do something, wanted this to be an experience that would help me be…. "better". My description is too weak, but I really am at a loss to fully explain.

As I was praying, I kept thinking that this event had something to do with the heart of the nation. Heart of the nation. Heart of the nation? Was that Washington, D. C.? Was that us in Washington(the participants at the event)? Was it the church? I wasn't sure, but those words kept coming to mind. I took out a fresh legal pad (you know, that stuff consultants carry around). I thought it must be important. I wanted to get back to my time with God. "I'll make a note of this, just a few thoughts...", I remember thinking to myself. I was in for a surprise.

As I began to write down those words, "Heart of the Nation", I knew there was something more. I have written poetry and lyrics before. I have even felt inspired to do so. Somehow this seemed different. I continued writing until the title selection of this work, "Heart of the Nation" was complete. However, I was still crying.

As I began to write the words, I felt sorrowful, and tears filled my eyes. I felt convicted for my own lack, my own sin, in the areas I was writing about. As I read and reread what was written, I wept. This went on for fifteen minutes or so. Finally, the tears ended and I put the poem in a manila folder. I thought, "This is for me and for everyone. This must be what the October 4th event is about". I filed the poem away thinking it was completed and that I was done. I was partially correct.

The next morning I arose early to have my quiet time with God. (NOTE: I'll try not to use too many clichés when telling my story, but phrases sometimes become clichés because they fit so well, as in this case, don't you think?) As I was reading and praying, I found my thoughts wandering over to the October 4th event again. As I began to pray in the Spirit, I could "see" in my mind's eye two men in long off-white gowns sitting on the steps of the Capitol, each holding a scythe. Within minutes I had written the second work in this book, "Warfare with the Ancients". Again I was crying. I began praying to God to ask what was happening, what were these writings? Moments later I came to understand that they were to be a part of a collection of thirty-one writings about the "Heart of the Nation".

What you hold in your hand and are now reading is the culmination of the 31 days I experienced, starting on September 16, 1997. I wrote at least one poem almost everyday. I found that if for some reason I would miss a day, the next day I would write two. At one point I discovered that if I allowed myself, I would just continue to write (mixed with weeping, singing, praying, and praising God). The most I ever wrote was four in one day. The longest I ever went without writing one was two days. As someone who has created other types of works for publication, I was amazed that in about one month a book went from nothing to being ready to distribute. However, that is not the most significant thing about this time period and this work.

What I came to discover was that what I was experiencing was only loosely associated with the event in Washington, D. C. "The Heart of the Nation" is about turning back to God. It is about families being restored. It is about putting off the ways of sin. You know, the deep down stuff that you think only you know about. Remember, if you are a Christian, Jesus gets to share your thoughts, the things you let your mind dwell upon. Makes you want to cry, doesn't it?

I discovered it was and is about me. It is about my family. It is about how God is waiting to show himself strong on behalf of all who will give up everything to follow Jesus. It is about how turning to God - humbling your heart, weeping for the lost, and refusing to participate in the world's dirge of ridicule and hatred of those that are different - will result in a new life. A new life in Christ for each one, for everyone, who calls upon Jesus.

So, what evidence do I have to make these statements?

Well, I do not want to take the time to give all of the details here – or this book would never be done! Following is a short list:

- On September 17, 1997, my consulting business kicked off in a substantial way.

- On September 27, 1997, my son accepted Jesus as his Savior. (My wife and I had the honor of praying with him).

- On September 28, 1997, my son prayed and asked God to go to Washington on October 4th. He went. (Not enough room here, but this was indeed a miracle!)

- On October 5, 1997, my youngest daughter rededicated her life to God at the alter in front of the church in response to a call for renewal by one of our pastors, Rev. Dale Turner.

- On October 5, 1997 my oldest daughter felt God "pressing" on her and she began to return to seeking God.

- Of course, there is this book.

- My wife has discovered a new and deeper relationship with Jesus than she has ever known.

- I have discovered a closer relationship to God than I have ever had. And I was allowed the honor of participating in creating the journey. You can, too.

I believe every Christian can share these same blessings in their life! God has helped me to find a deeper understanding of repentance and holiness. He continues to work this work in me. I believe that this book can help Christians find their way to serving Jesus as they always desired, and to participate in creating that path, that journey, of service. I believe that it can help those who do not believe, or who have fallen into unbelief, to turn their hearts toward home, to Jesus the Messiah who is Lord of Lords, King of Kings, and the Ancient of Days. I can only pray that you receive a blessing from this book and that your life be richly rewarded.

Before you go on, I do want to make one thing very clear: No one needs this book to find Jesus or to get themselves and their families closer to God. This book is NOT a substitute for your personal one-on-one contact and friendship with the Father, Jesus, or the Holy Spirit. It may help you understand what I have experienced, and help you to find your own experience with the One True God. If you can experience even a small portion of the blessing that God has bestowed and is bestowing upon me and my family from this material, then I shall count myself honored at being allowed to be a part of that. If you have this book because you think you need it to know God, please return it.

In the following section of the book I will offer some suggestions on how to get the most out of these materials. How do you make your way home? You and God create your journey. My suggestions are based on my own journey, my own trek to a deeper, closer relationship with Jesus. Your journey will be different. But it will be your journey to, and with, Jesus. May it be a fruitful one. God bless you!

How To Use This Book

Chapter 2

How To Use This Book

"Heart of the Nation" is meant to be a help to <u>you</u> to develop <u>your</u> relationship with God. Think of it as a journey, an exciting adventure in which you are the traveler and the explorer. As God has written, "….work out your own salvation with fear and trembling…" - *Philippians 2:12.* Every Christian is responsible to God for their own walk with Him. If we seek him with a humble heart, He will give us the power to live holy unto Him (Philippians 1:6 and 2:13).

Though written in a format that you may not be accustomed to, this book can provide you with enough structure to help you develop a sustained effort in your seeking God. It also allows enough freedom to make your journey towards Jesus and His holiness <u>*your*</u> journey and not a "canned approach". It requires your participation to fully realize the blessing you can receive. As a result of my journey, I received a deeper and clearer walk with God, my family restored to Jesus, and a blessing on the "work of my hands". What you receive will be what you and God create.

There are 31 writings in this book, of which one is clearly incomplete (more about that later). These writings appear on the odd numbered pages - the right-hand side of the book. On the pages facing these works are some tools to help you become involved in creating your journey. The tools are: Prayers and Praise, Scripture Readings, Reflections, and Requests. Use these tools in conjunction with the readings, one each day for 31 days. You will be creating your own unique journal of what God does in your life during your journey.

Begin by praising God the Father for His greatness, and praying, asking God to bless your time you are dedicating to Him. Read the Scripture Readings. You are encouraged to substitute other scripture readings if you feel it appropriate, <u>but make sure to write down what you read if it is different from what is suggested.</u>

Next, read the writing for that day. Think about what is being communicated through the writings. Some offer the chance to examine your life. Others offer words to use to praise God. Still others offer a chance to reflect on the difference between the world of Jesus and the world of sin. What is important is your prayer and praise to God, the reading of the scriptures, and what the thoughts offered in these writings reveals to _you_.

Use the Reflections area to record what is important to you for your journey. Perhaps repentance, praise, or thankfulness. It is important to capture at least one thought in this area.

Then lastly, record your Requests. Use your own discretion and the leading of the Holy Spirit. Remember why you are doing this work when you record your requests. Whatever your request is, the answering of it should result in God being glorified. Enough said.

If at all possible, avoid reading through the material for the joy of reading without doing the work to create and record your personal journey. As you move through this book, you may want to read ahead. Going beyond one journal entry each day can be taxing on you, your family, or other time commitments. Again, make certain that enthusiasm to deepen your relationship with God does not interfere with other commitments that He has already given to you. I found it necessary, in fact exciting, to rise up early and pursue the journey, a practice that I still pursue.

On the thirty-first day you will celebrate the completion of your journey. It may take more time than the previous days, so be sure to plan ahead. You will notice that the last writing is considerably shorter that the others. From each of the previous thirty days select at least one item and write it into the space provided for the thirty-first writing. This will become your personal recap of the journey. After you complete this writing, read it. Meditate on what God has shown you. Praise Him out loud. Wave the book and your writing over your head as you praise Him as an offering, an act of thankfulness, for His mercy toward you and your family.

And last of all, never quit. After you have completed this 31 day journey to a closer walk with God, I believe you will find as I have that you never, never want to lose such a sweet and precious relationship with the Master and Creator.

"...And as I looked upon the multitude, I heard Jesus say, 'We'll see... It can be... We shall see.'"

To God be the glory. Let the journey begin....

Your Journey Begins...

Chapter 3

PRAYERS AND PRAISE - Go before the Father in Jesus' name. What are you thankful for? What do you want to praise God for? Write it down here: _____

_____

_____

_____

_____

SCRIPTURE READINGS - Read the scriptures first, then the writing. If you substitute your own scripture selections, make a note of them here:

> Proverbs 1   Matthew 25:31-46
>
> Joel 1:14
>
> Ephesians 5:15-16

REFLECTIONS - If you were to write down one or two thoughts on what these scripture readings and the writing here means to you, they would be (write them down in the space provided): _____

_____

_____

_____

_____

_____

REQUESTS - Write down what you want to request of God at this point in your journey. _____

_____

_____

Heart of the Nation

Stand in the Gap, October 4, 1997

Is this the heart of the nation?
Is this the sign of the times?
Will this be the generation
That turns the heart and mind
To the Master and Creator,
To the Truth that sets men free?
As I looked upon the multitude,
I heard Jesus say, "We'll see."

Do you scoff at the homosexual
instead of weep with him, side by side?
Do you turn your back on the poor
because you have your pride?
And have you spoken to your child
in a way that hardens the heart?
If you answered yes to these,
now is the time to start.

Prayers, Praise, and Reflections - Make additional notes here:

You start by falling to your knees

By crying out, "My God,

Not only upon the least of these

But upon your name, Jesus, I trod."

Are we the heart of the nation?

Are we the sign of the times?

Will we be the generation

That turns the heart and mind

To the Master and Creator,

To the Truth that sets men free?

As I looked upon the multitude,

I heard Jesus say, "We'll see."

As I stood at the nation's doorstep and beheld men, free,

Jesus pointed to the sightseers, one of them was me.

Caught up in splendor and beauty of days gone by

Losing precious time, but I said "Oh no, Lord, not I."

Jesus turned to look at me, I began to weep,

Reflected in Loving Eyes was the sin I tried to keep.

Trembling, "Please forgive me," was all I could say

Falling, He caught me and said,

"You started afresh today."

Prayers, Praise, and Reflections - Make additional notes here:

Are you the heart of the nation?

Are you the sign of the times?

Will you be the generation

That turns hearts and minds

To the Master and Creator,

To the Truth that sets men free?

As I looked upon the multitude,

I heard Jesus say, "We'll see."

As I looked upon the multitude,

I heard Jesus say, "It can be."

And as I looked upon the multitude,

I heard Jesus say, "We shall see."

PRAYERS AND PRAISE - Go before the Father in Jesus' name. What are you thankful for? What do you want to praise God for? Write it down here: _____

_____

_____

_____

_____

SCRIPTURE READINGS - Read the scriptures first, then the writing. If you substitute your own scripture selections, make a note of them here:

     Proverbs 2   Matthew 14:30-33

     Psalm 20:1-2, 6-9

     Ephesians 6:12

REFLECTIONS - If you were to write down one or two thoughts on what these scripture readings and the writing here means to you, they would be (write them down in the space provided): _____

_____

_____

_____

_____

_____

_____

REQUESTS - Write down what you want to request of God at this point in your journey. _____

_____

_____

_____

Warfare with the Ancients

I saw two ancients sitting,
Each with a sickle in his hand.
They cried "Feed me, Feed me!",
Reaping souls from across the land.
I wondered at their presence,
Who were these men in flowing gowns?
As I drew near to them I noticed
Their garments bore the names of many towns.
And each town whose name they wore,
I knew at once, from the news.
In those towns evil walked freely,
Searching for the weak to abuse.

Stunned at the sight of such evil
I wondered, "How could this be?
Here I am in the nation's capital.
Here I am in the land of the free."

We had come to pray
To seek God's face, hour upon hour,
Then suddenly it came to me,
These were rulers of the air, principalities and powers.

Prayers, Praise, and Reflections - Make additional notes here:

They had come to Washington
To see what havoc they could wreak.
I knew something must be done -
I went up to them to speak,
"You will have to leave this place.
We Christians have come to pray."
Looking at each other they arose,
As if they would just walk away.

Pleased at their quick retreat
I pondered, "How do they abide?
Here I am in the nation's capital.
Here I am in a land with pride."

Faster than the glint from steel
They spun 'round with sickles swinging
Throwing words as if they were darts,
Death and Hell in their weapons singing.
I froze as they moved toward us crying,
"You fools! Who do you think you are!?
In all our taking, we shall take you, too!
DID YOU THINK YOU WOULD GET VERY FAR!!!?"
My palms grew cold and sweaty,
I felt my heart begin to wrench.
They were swinging their sickles at me.
Death filled the air, from their robes, with a stench.

Prayers, Praise, and Reflections - Make additional notes here:

_____

_____

_____

_____

_____

_____

_____

_____

_____

_____

_____

_____

_____

_____

_____

_____

_____

_____

_____

_____

_____

_____

_____

_____

_____

Gripped by terror of impending doom,
Of evil's flooding sea,
There, in the nation's capital.
I cried out, "Jesus, save us! Save me!"

As I fell to the ground in fear
I saw Jesus step in and take the blow
"Perhaps I Am the One you seek,
Perhaps it is My blood you wish to know".
As His words peeled forth
The ancients began to groan.
"Stop, stop, we can't stand it!"
But to me, it was the most beautiful tone.
"Say nothing of the red stream!",
They cried with a hand over each ear.
Jesus turned, offering me His hand,
He said, "It is finished. Do not fear."

In that moment I knew
A refreshing I cannot explain,
There we were in the nation's capital
There we were in the latter rain.

Prayers, Praise, and Reflections - Make additional notes here:

Jesus raised us to our feet
Healed our wounds and removed the darts
"Do not let them take the land," He said,
"Humble yourselves, and your hearts.
I have given you all a ministry,
You are my ambassadors upon this earth,
Defend the land with your words:
To the heavy hearted give mirth,
To the sick and wounded,
Bring healing, and sight to the blind.
And always remember, I Am with you,
None can take you, you are Mine."

And we all were in that place
With one accord and voice,
"May Jesus' blood cover our capital,
In Jesus name let the land rejoice!"

And there was a peaceful joy
A space for us to stand and see
A nation and its capital begin to turn
To the Truth that truly sets men free.

PRAYERS AND PRAISE - Go before the Father in Jesus' name. What are you thankful for? What do you want to praise God for? Write it down here: _____

_____

_____

_____

_____

SCRIPTURE READINGS - Read the scriptures first, then the writing. If you substitute your own scripture selections, make a note of them here:

Proverbs 3   Psalm 95:6-8

Jeremiah 1:1-10

Hebrews 6:6

REFLECTIONS - If you were to write down one or two thoughts on what these scripture readings and the writing here means to you, they would be (write them down in the space provided): _____

_____

_____

_____

_____

_____

_____

REQUESTS - Write down what you want to request of God at this point in your journey. _____

_____

_____

Humility, True and False

"My Lord, Jesus, I am greatly grieved
For it is Your precious life I've received
Yet as I think of my life, my deeds
I don't see a garden, I only see weeds."
Then Jesus smiled, with that penetrating look
He spoke quietly, "Put this in your book."
And He reached out His hands, taking mine,
"You are all branches, I Am the Vine.
Each time you each dig up your sinful past
Or repeat those same sins, saying 'It's the last',
Know only this, with each thought, word, and deed
Of refreshed sin, you nail Me up again to bleed."

Then He looked at our clasped hands, and I did, too.
Suddenly, I noticed, His hands were bleeding anew.
Startled I looked up, what I saw pierced me through,
It was tears in His eyes, "There's one for each of you."

I began shaking, my tears did erupt
With those blood drenched hands, Jesus held me up.
I wept, and I wept, till I felt empty inside
I said, "Jesus, forgive me." He nodded,
"At last you have died."

Prayers, Praise, and Reflections - Make additional notes here:

He embraced me and told me, "Now that you know,
you must tell others. Tell them of the flow.
Of my blood and My tears, that they, too, may cry.
Through their weeping and praying they, too, can die."
And as he held me there, close,
He kissed my cheek.
"From now on when I tell you to, you must speak."
I nodded, sheepishly, but He gently lifted my chin
"Have you so quickly forgotten?",
His eyes pierced me within.

This time, I smiled, "No, Lord, I'll always remember."
I saw His eyes smile, each like a glowing ember.
"Good." He said, "Let this be the beginning, the start.
Tell them to serve Me they must humble their heart
And ask them why, if they love Me as they say they do
Why are their bibles dusty,
their prayer carpets mildewed?"

PRAYERS AND PRAISE - Go before the Father in Jesus' name. What are you thankful for? What do you want to praise God for? Write it down here: _____

_____

_____

_____

_____

SCRIPTURE READINGS - Read the scriptures first, then the writing. If you substitute your own scripture selections, make a note of them here:

Proverbs 4   Matthew 25:14-30

Joel 2:12-17

Matthew 23:2-12

REFLECTIONS - If you were to write down one or two thoughts on what these scripture readings and the writing here means to you, they would be (write them down in the space provided): _____

_____

_____

_____

_____

_____

_____

REQUESTS - Write down what you want to request of God at this point in your journey. _____

_____

_____

_____

How Sacred is Your assembly?

How sacred is your assembly?
How many of you believe,
That Jesus is the answer
To those burdens for which you now grieve?
Before any answer,
Before you raise your hand,
If we asked your neighbors,
Your family, do they know where you stand?

You can pray in the nation's capital,
Sing, prophesy, or moan.
The true test of conviction
Is who you are when you're at home.
Before any answer,
Placing hands on your hips,
If we asked the poor and needy,
Would your name be upon their lips?

Humble yourselves, humble yourselves,
Step back into the crowd.
Give Jesus room to work.
In secret give your gifts.
Resist the haughty and the proud.

PRAYERS AND PRAISE - Go before the Father in Jesus' name. What are you thankful for? What do you want to praise God for? Write it down here: _____

_____

_____

_____

_____

SCRIPTURE READINGS - Read the scriptures first, then the writing. If you substitute your own scripture selections, make a note of them here:

> Proverbs 5   Luke 20:17-18
>
> Hosea 3:1-5
>
> Ephesians 6:13-18

REFLECTIONS - If you were to write down one or two thoughts on what these scripture readings and the writing here means to you, they would be (write them down in the space provided): _____

_____

_____

_____

_____

_____

_____

REQUESTS - Write down what you want to request of God at this point in your journey. _____

_____

_____

_____

Hosea's Wife

You have given yourself to many others,
But now is the time of turning.
Put away the sin that enslaves,
The evil that was within you burning.

"I have given you power.
Do not walk away.
Take up the shield of faith,
Turn while it is called today.

The God of the fathers has seen you,
He knows of the evil you do.
"That Prophet" has bought you with a price,
He has paid for each and every one of you.

"I have given you healing.
Do not walk away.
Speak with the sword, the Word,
Heal while it is called today."

Prayers, Praise, and Reflections - Make additional notes here:

Jesus is "that Prophet" foretold,
Your sins are those of the harlot,
Turn from your adulterous ways,
Your sin cleansed by the flowing scarlet.

"I have given you life
Do not walk away.
Break yourself upon the Rock
Speak life while it has called today."

PRAYERS AND PRAISE - Go before the Father in Jesus' name. What are you thankful for? What do you want to praise God for? Write it down here: _____

_____

_____

_____

_____

SCRIPTURE READINGS - Read the scriptures first, then the writing. If you substitute your own scripture selections, make a note of them here:

> Proverbs 6
>
> Hosea 4:6
>
> John 8:30-32

REFLECTIONS - If you were to write down one or two thoughts on what these scripture readings and the writing here means to you, they would be (write them down in the space provided): _____

_____

_____

_____

_____

_____

_____

REQUESTS - Write down what you want to request of God at this point in your journey. _____

_____

_____

_____

How do You Change a nation?

How do you change a nation?
Whose heart has grown cold?
How do you change the future?
Has the story already been told?
Has the story already been told?
Death and violence, sadness and grief
Everywhere you turn, evidence of the thief.
I grow angry at the desolation I see before my eyes.
I weep at the tribulation I know will soon rise.
Where is the power to set a nation free?
Jesus said, "If each one knows the Truth,
the Truth will make men free."

How do you change a person
Whose heart has grown cold?
How do you change their future
To be added to the fold?
To be added to the fold?
Death and violence, sadness and grief
Everywhere you turn, evidence of the thief.
Where is the power to set a person free?
Jesus said, "If each one knows the Truth,
the Truth will make them free."

PRAYERS AND PRAISE - Go before the Father in Jesus' name. What are you thankful for? What do you want to praise God for? Write it down here: _____

_____

_____

_____

_____

SCRIPTURE READINGS - Read the scriptures first, then the writing. If you substitute your own scripture selections, make a note of them here:

     Proverbs 7   I Peter 2:5, 9-17

     Proverbs 16:33

     Joel 2:13

REFLECTIONS - If you were to write down one or two thoughts on what these scripture readings and the writing here means to you, they would be (write them down in the space provided): _____

_____

_____

_____

_____

_____

_____

REQUESTS - Write down what you want to request of God at this point in your journey. _____

_____

_____

_____

Rend

If you come to pray for a nation,
Looking to change this generation,
Looking to change the hearts and minds,
Of those that have fallen
By crying out to Jesus and callin'
On His wondrous name, in these desperate times.
Start a trend!
Start a holy wave!
Do not bend,
Like others behave.
Be a holy people,
A priesthood without wrinkle or spot.

The change you seek starts with you.
Though hard to hear, you know its true.
For Jesus is looking for a holy bride.
Crush yourself and be broken
Upon the Rock; give all, not a token.
Confess your sins to the One in whom you confide.
Stand, defend!
Stand up and be brave!
Tear and rend,
Put sin in the grave.
Be a holy nation,
A people trusting God for their lot.

PRAYERS AND PRAISE - Go before the Father in Jesus' name. What are you thankful for? What do you want to praise God for? Write it down here: _____

_____

_____

_____

_____

_____

SCRIPTURE READINGS - Read the scriptures first, then the writing. If you substitute your own scripture selections, make a note of them here:

    Proverbs 8

    II Chronicles 16:9

    Psalm 33:18-19

REFLECTIONS - If you were to write down one or two thoughts on what these scripture readings and the writing here means to you, they would be (write them down in the space provided): _____

_____

_____

_____

_____

_____

_____

REQUESTS - Write down what you want to request of God at this point in your journey. _____

_____

_____

_____

Where are the Warriors?

You say you are sad for your country's direction,
And you wish people would not practice sin,
But each morning when you rise, or nightly sleep,
Have you asked God for more than your soul to keep?

Where are the warriors?
Where have they gone?
No champions among us?
It seems like so long.

When the eye if the Lord searches to defend,
Does He see you with knees bent,
another message to send?
As the lost and lonely move closer to the fire,
Do you stand to deliver, or join the funeral pyre?

Where are the warriors?
Where can they be?
The champions among us?
Is that you and me?

Prayers, Praise, and Reflections - Make additional notes here:

_____

_____

_____

_____

_____

_____

_____

_____

_____

_____

_____

_____

_____

_____

_____

_____

_____

_____

_____

_____

_____

_____

_____

So if you are ready to stand straight and tall,
To weep with those who mourn and don't know it at all.
If you can shed at least one precious tear,
Then you're ready to heal them, and drive out their fear.

We are the warriors,
At least we can be.
With Jesus among us
We can change what we see.

PRAYERS AND PRAISE - Go before the Father in Jesus' name. What are you thankful for? What do you want to praise God for? Write it down here: _____

_____

_____

_____

_____

SCRIPTURE READINGS - Read the scriptures first, then the writing. If you substitute your own scripture selections, make a note of them here:

Proverbs 9   Philippians 1:27-28

Romans 8:1

Ephesians 4:29-32

REFLECTIONS - If you were to write down one or two thoughts on what these scripture readings and the writing here means to you, they would be (write them down in the space provided): _____

_____

_____

_____

_____

_____

_____

REQUESTS - Write down what you want to request of God at this point in your journey. _____

_____

_____

_____

Humility Shows

Your friends, your children,
Those you work with and your wife,
Hear all the words you say,
See all the actions in your life.
Do they hear a humble man,
Or is the cart before the horse?
One thing is for sure,
When they hear you, Jesus must be the source.
When they hear you, Jesus must be the source.

Your friends, your children,
Those you work with and your wife,
Hear all the words you say,
See all the actions in your life.
Do they see a humble man,
Or is the horse after the cart?
One thing is for sure,
When they see you, they need to see Jesus' heart.
When they see you, they need to see Jesus' heart.

PRAYERS AND PRAISE - Go before the Father in Jesus' name. What are you thankful for? What do you want to praise God for? Write it down here: _____

_____

_____

_____

_____

SCRIPTURE READINGS - Read the scriptures first, then the writing. If you substitute your own scripture selections, make a note of them here:

> **Proverbs 10**
> **John 10:25-30**
> **Acts 16:31-34**

REFLECTIONS - If you were to write down one or two thoughts on what these scripture readings and the writing here means to you, they would be (write them down in the space provided): _____

_____

_____

_____

_____

_____

_____

REQUESTS - Write down what you want to request of God at this point in your journey. _____

_____

_____

_____

Nothing Shall Ever
Tear this Child from My Hand

I don't now recall
exactly how it began.
The storm had been raging,
the water came over the dam.
I saw my child fastened
securely in her chair.
What was meant for safe keeping
had become a death trap then and there.
I struggled to release her,
waters rushing from the dam, broke.
I tried desperately to pull her free -
as the waters covered her, I awoke.

Winds whistle and waters roar,
Death and violence behind every door.
Though I may be overcome,
'tis here I take my stand.
Nothing shall ever, ever,
tear this child from my hand.

Prayers, Praise, and Reflections - Make additional notes here:

I was trembling and crying,
I had seen my greatest fear.
I could not rescue my child,
the one I held so dear.
I stumbled back from her room,
her face shining in a moon beam.
With tearful determination,
I dove back in my dream.

Reliving the same peril,
from only the moment before,
I pushed through the waters,
to the open car door.
As the waters rushed in from behind,
I summoned all my power,
I cried aloud "Jesus!"
"Save her in this hour!"
With a sudden inhuman force,
I pulled her loose, holding her over my head.
The waters overwhelmed me,
Face down and floating - I was dead.
Clasping my daughter's chair in my hands,
we floated downstream above the tide.
My child was pulled ashore by others,
and I had won, though I had died.

Prayers, Praise, and Reflections - Make additional notes here:

Winds whistle and waters roar,
Death and violence behind every door.
Though I may be overcome,
'tis here I take my stand.
Nothing shall ever, ever,
tear this child from my hand.

Many years have past since then,
lately she and I have grown apart.
Sometimes I become a raging storm,
although I don't want to in my heart.
And life's evils flow like floods,
from the broken dam of Hell,
Till the overwhelming tide of troubles,
do more damage than one can tell.
As I thought about the words we spoke,
about the actions and tears,
I was trembling and crying,
I had seen my greatest fear.

That's when Jesus spoke to me.
In a still small voice he said,
"I still love you both.
That's why I died and bled.

Prayers, Praise, and Reflections - Make additional notes here:

A perfect father you will never be,
nor her the perfect child,
Still you can each be free,
And remember," He said as He smiled,

"Winds whistle and waters roar,
Death and violence behind every door.
Though you may be overcome,
'tis here I take My stand
Nothing shall ever, ever,
tear your child from My hand.

Oh, no,

Nothing shall ever, ever,
tear your child,
No, nothing shall ever, ever
tear you, child,
from My hand."

PRAYERS AND PRAISE - Go before the Father in Jesus' name. What are you thankful for? What do you want to praise God for? Write it down here: _____

_____

_____

_____

_____

SCRIPTURE READINGS - Read the scriptures first, then the writing. If you substitute your own scripture selections, make a note of them here:

      Proverbs 11   Matthew 24:45-51

      Psalm 51:10-13

      Joel 2:28-29

REFLECTIONS - If you were to write down one or two thoughts on what these scripture readings and the writing here means to you, they would be (write them down in the space provided): _____

_____

_____

_____

_____

_____

_____

REQUESTS - Write down what you want to request of God at this point in your journey. _____

_____

_____

Dusty Moments

Make the most of each moment.
Make a dream come true.
Make your life a memory,
Of the day Jesus died for you.

How much dust lies on the memory
of the day when you first called His Name?
Do you commune with God every day,
or have you taken yourself out of the game?
Just as sure as this life
is not a game of chance,
each one must make a choice.
With whom will you dance this dance?

Make the most of each moment.
Make a dream come true.
Make your life a memory,
Of the day Jesus died for you.

I'll make the most of each moment.
Make a dream come true.
Make my life a memory,
Of the day Jesus died for me and you.

PRAYERS AND PRAISE - Go before the Father in Jesus' name. What are you thankful for? What do you want to praise God for? Write it down here: _____

_____

_____

_____

_____

SCRIPTURE READINGS - Read the scriptures first, then the writing. If you substitute your own scripture selections, make a note of them here:

Proverbs 12   Luke 4:40

Psalm 103:1-5 Luke 9:1-2

Matthew 18:19

REFLECTIONS - If you were to write down one or two thoughts on what these scripture readings and the writing here means to you, they would be (write them down in the space provided): _____

_____

_____

_____

_____

_____

REQUESTS - Write down what you want to request of God at this point in your journey. _____

_____

_____

Two Warriors, One Voice

Two warriors standing,
Next to the deep blue sea.
Two warriors standing,
It was Jesus and me.

Prepared to fight
What came across the waters.
Prepared to fight
For the sons and daughters.

Two warriors standing,
Next to the deep blue sea.
Two warriors standing,
It was Jesus and me.

With the Word, a sword,
Together, we spoke healing.
With the Word, a sword,
Power to send death reeling.

Two warriors standing,
Next to the deep blue sea.
Two warriors standing,
It was Jesus and me.

PRAYERS AND PRAISE - Go before the Father in Jesus' name. What are you thankful for? What do you want to praise God for? Write it down here: _____

_____

_____

_____

_____

SCRIPTURE READINGS - Read the scriptures first, then the writing. If you substitute your own scripture selections, make a note of them here:

> Proverbs 13
> Proverbs 20:25
> Luke 14:25-33

REFLECTIONS - If you were to write down one or two thoughts on what these scripture readings and the writing here means to you, they would be (write them down in the space provided): _____

_____

_____

_____

_____

_____

_____

REQUESTS - Write down what you want to request of God at this point in your journey. _____

_____

_____

_____

Count the Cost

Before you go after a nation,
Or a town, city, or state,
Sit for a moment, clear your mind,
Count the cost - freedom.   Meditate.

Everyone wants to cheer the winner.
Everyone wants to win the prize.
Sometimes in the lust for battle
There are a few things unrealized.
There is a price to pay for sin.
That ultimate price was paid, it's true,
But if you want to turn a nation,
The price to be paid, is you.

Before you go after a nation,
Or a town, city, or state,
Sit for a moment, clear your mind,
Count the cost - freedom.   Meditate.

Prayers, Praise, and Reflections - Make additional notes here:

Everyone wants to cheer the winner.
Everyone want to win the "gold".
Sometimes in the lust for battle
There are some things that go untold.
The cost to be counted is your life -
Your comforts, time, and emotions.
Surrender all you have and are.
Never stop. Live your devotions.

Everyone wants to cheer the winner.
Everyone wants to win the praise.
Now you know, winning means dying.
Surrender to Jesus, the Ancient of Days.

PRAYERS AND PRAISE - Go before the Father in Jesus' name. What are you thankful for? What do you want to praise God for? Write it down here: _____

_____

_____

_____

_____

SCRIPTURE READINGS - Read the scriptures first, then the writing. If you substitute your own scripture selections, make a note of them here:

>   Proverbs 14
>   Proverbs 2:1-4
>   John 10:1-5

REFLECTIONS - If you were to write down one or two thoughts on what these scripture readings and the writing here means to you, they would be (write them down in the space provided): _____

_____

_____

_____

_____

_____

_____

REQUESTS - Write down what you want to request of God at this point in your journey. _____

_____

_____

_____

Phone Call

Can you hear me when I speak?
Do you know My voice well?
If I called you on the telephone
Would you be able to tell?
A friend is someone you spend time with,
Share tears of joy and pain.
If someone asked you about our friendship,
What could you tell him? Would you have to refrain?

I have called My chosen people,
But you have to pick up the phone.
If I called you to help the needy,
Would I hear, "Sorry, I'm not home . . . ?"

If you listen, you will hear Me,
You have to try with all your heart.
If My words were nuggets of gold,
How long would it take you to start?

Prayers, Praise, and Reflections - Make additional notes here:

_____

_____

_____

_____

_____

_____

_____

_____

_____

_____

_____

_____

_____

_____

_____

_____

_____

_____

_____

_____

_____

_____

_____

_____

You can start by rising early,
Wherever you are lift your voice.
Seek Truth with everything within you,
I love to hear you praise and rejoice.

I have called My holy priest hood,
A precious bride, unblemished and true.
Search your heart and listen closely
Treasure My works, I'll give them to you.

PRAYERS AND PRAISE - Go before the Father in Jesus' name. What are you thankful for? What do you want to praise God for? Write it down here: _____

_____

_____

_____

_____

SCRIPTURE READINGS - Read the scriptures first, then the writing. If you substitute your own scripture selections, make a note of them here:

Proverbs 15   Matthew 15:22-28

Nehemiah 4:17-19

Proverbs 22:6

REFLECTIONS - If you were to write down one or two thoughts on what these scripture readings and the writing here means to you, they would be (write them down in the space provided): _____

_____

_____

_____

_____

_____

_____

REQUESTS - Write down what you want to request of God at this point in your journey. _____

_____

_____

_____

Wall of Prayer

Jesus I know you love me.
You are worth of every praise.
You are my loving Savior.
You are the Ancient of Days.

As I look at my life and my family,
I now see the error of my ways.
For I have let so much time pass,
Precious moments, many lost days.
I thought about times I worked long,
Chasing one more dollar to which I could hold.
Now I see, as I am looking back,
Sharing love and prayer is the only true gold.

Jesus I know you love me.
You are worthy of every praise.
You are my loving Savior.
You are the Ancient of Days.

As I stood weeping for my family,
Saddened at the days passed by,
Jesus came to me, raising me up,
He wiped every tear from my eyes.

Prayers, Praise, and Reflections - Make additional notes here:

_____

_____

_____

_____

_____

_____

_____

_____

_____

_____

_____

_____

_____

_____

_____

_____

_____

_____

_____

_____

_____

_____

_____

_____

_____

_____

"I can give you power to change your family,
Turn your sadness into tears of joy,
If you speak and do the things I tell you,
I'll deliver your wife, daughters, and boy."

Jesus I know you love me.
You are worthy of every praise.
You are my loving Savior.
You are the Ancient of Days.

"Make for yourself a wall with faith.
Write down every single prayer.
Remember always, pray in the Spirit.
And remember, I'll always be there.
Let your children read My words.
Record the needs, no matter how small,
Track the victories, the answered prayers,
You'll see My thumb print upon your wall."

Jesus we know you love us.
You are worthy of every praise.
You are our loving Savior.
You are the Ancient of Days.

PRAYERS AND PRAISE - Go before the Father in Jesus' name. What are you thankful for? What do you want to praise God for? Write it down here: _____

_____

_____

_____

_____

SCRIPTURE READINGS - Read the scriptures first, then the writing. If you substitute your own scripture selections, make a note of them here:

> Proverbs 16   Romans 8:26-30
> Psalm 46:1-3
> Romans 7:23

REFLECTIONS - If you were to write down one or two thoughts on what these scripture readings and the writing here means to you, they would be (write them down in the space provided): _____

_____

_____

_____

_____

_____

REQUESTS - Write down what you want to request of God at this point in your journey. _____

_____

_____

Battleground of the Mind

Sometimes I worry, though I'm not sure why.
I know that You love me, that's why you died.
I think too much about my children's needs,
When I do, I forget, it's You who intercedes.

Thank you Jesus,
You are the All in All.
Thank you Jesus,
For giving me the call.

Thoughts sometimes come to me
from out of the blue.
They crowd me, they shove me,
make me forget about you.
When accusations and lies
loudly crowd into my head,
"In Jesus' name, be gone!"
is all that need be said.

Thank you Jesus,
For giving me the call.
Thank you Jesus,
You are the All in All.

PRAYERS AND PRAISE - Go before the Father in Jesus' name. What are you thankful for? What do you want to praise God for? Write it down here: _____

_____

_____

_____

_____

SCRIPTURE READINGS - Read the scriptures first, then the writing. If you substitute your own scripture selections, make a note of them here:

Proverbs 17   James 5:16-18

Hosea 1:2

Hosea 4:11-12

REFLECTIONS - If you were to write down one or two thoughts on what these scripture readings and the writing here means to you, they would be (write them down in the space provided): _____

_____

_____

_____

_____

_____

REQUESTS - Write down what you want to request of God at this point in your journey. _____

_____

_____

_____

Spirit of Harlotry

The harlot sits at the gate.
Just when you think it's too late,
You realize its not a woman at all
It's a Legion, it's coming wall to wall.

Cry out to Jesus!
Speak His Holy Word!
Make a joyful noise!
In high places be heard!
In high places be heard!

Enemies of God, though many,
Not a one can stand, not any.
When a holy priest speaks the Truth in love,
Jesus seals it with power from above.

Cry out to Jesus!
Speak His Holy Word!
Make a joyful noise!
In high places be heard!
In high places be heard!

Effective means it comes to pass,
Not like the wind that does not last.
Fervent as water in the pot boiling,
Confess your sin, spend time in prayer toiling.

Cry out to Jesus!
Speak His holy Name!
Lay hands on the sick,
None will ever be the same!

PRAYERS AND PRAISE - Go before the Father in Jesus' name. What are you thankful for? What do you want to praise God for? Write it down here: _____

_____

_____

_____

_____

SCRIPTURE READINGS - Read the scriptures first, then the writing. If you substitute your own scripture selections, make a note of them here:

> Proverbs 18
> Psalm 2:1-6
> Acts 4:24-32

REFLECTIONS - If you were to write down one or two thoughts on what these scripture readings and the writing here means to you, they would be (write them down in the space provided): _____

_____

_____

_____

_____

_____

_____

REQUESTS - Write down what you want to request of God at this point in your journey. _____

_____

_____

_____

Heathen Rage

Heathen:
"Make the Truth a lie!
Make the Truth a lie!"
You can hear the multitude chanting.
"Have you come with them?
Tell us! Are you with Him?"
Fervently the crowd is ranting.

Believers:
Rejoice! Lift up your voice,
Your deliverance is in your speaking
Rejoice! Lift up your voice,
Fill your words with love reeking.

Heathen:
"Why do you plague us?
Why do you plague us?!?"
You can hear the multitude roaring.
"Will you never leave?
Speak! Why must we believe?!?"
Now you have an opening, a mooring.

Believers:
Rejoice! Lift up your voice,
"Jesus you're worthy of honor and praise."
Rejoice! Lift up your voice,
"All worship and honor to the Ancient of Days!"

Prayers, Praise, and Reflections - Make additional notes here:

_____

_____

_____

_____

_____

_____

_____

_____

_____

_____

_____

_____

_____

_____

_____

_____

_____

_____

_____

_____

_____

_____

_____

_____

_____

And the multitude was quieted,
As "That Prophet" healed their land.
You are His servants now,
Power is in speaking and your hand.

Rejoice! Lift up your voice,
Your deliverance is in your speaking!
Rejoice! Lift up your voice,
Fill your words with love reeking.

PRAYERS AND PRAISE - Go before the Father in Jesus' name. What are you thankful for? What do you want to praise God for? Write it down here: _____

_____

_____

_____

_____

SCRIPTURE READINGS - Read the scriptures first, then the writing. If you substitute your own scripture selections, make a note of them here:

> Proverbs 19   Hebrew 11:1-3
>
> Psalm 144:1
>
> Habakkuk 3:4

REFLECTIONS - If you were to write down one or two thoughts on what these scripture readings and the writing here means to you, they would be (write them down in the space provided): _____

_____

_____

_____

_____

_____

_____

REQUESTS - Write down what you want to request of God at this point in your journey. _____

_____

_____

_____

Take the Land

Fingers of light,
Weapons of war,
Hold fast the land,
Give ground no more!

The day has past.
You're not a child.
In evil's face
Do not be mild!

Take the land, take the land
Praise God, rejoice!
In your hand, in your hand
Power from your voice,
Power from your voice.

Land is not earth.
Bullets aren't power.
The nation's the people,
Souls added each hour.
Time is now short.
The day at hand!
Seeds sewn from speaking with faith
Humble hearts, the land.

PRAYERS AND PRAISE - Go before the Father in Jesus' name. What are you thankful for? What do you want to praise God for? Write it down here: _____

_____

_____

_____

_____

SCRIPTURE READINGS - Read the scriptures first, then the writing. If you substitute your own scripture selections, make a note of them here:

> Proverbs 20
>
> Psalm 113
>
> Matthew 6:9-18

REFLECTIONS - If you were to write down one or two thoughts on what these scripture readings and the writing here means to you, they would be (write them down in the space provided): _____

_____

_____

_____

_____

_____

_____

REQUESTS - Write down what you want to request of God at this point in your journey. _____

_____

_____

_____

The Lord's Praise

We come together to seek our Father,
Who in heaven resides.
We praise the Name of Jesus our Savior,
Whose kingdom with us abides.

Alleluia, Alleluia!
Your kingdom and Your Word abide.
Alleluia, Alleluia!
We fear nothing. Jesus, right by our side.

We ask You, Father, send us Your presence,
What we need now, provide.
Give us your Spirit, indwell us and fill us,
Let Your kingdom in us abide.

Alleluia, Alleluia!
Your kingdom and Your Word abide.
Alleluia, Alleluia!
Power to love others, Holy Spirit inside.

Forgive us, oh God, for our sins against You,
Cleanse away bitterness and pride.
Give us a heart to forgive those around us,
Let Your kingdom on earth abide.

Prayers, Praise, and Reflections - Make additional notes here:

Alleluia, Alleluia
Your kingdom and Your Word abide
Alleluia, Alleluia
Your glory will forever abide.

Come to us, come to us
Let Your kingdom and Your Word abide
Fill us, Lord, indwell us
That Your Kingdom on earth abides.

PRAYERS AND PRAISE - Go before the Father in Jesus' name. What are you thankful for? What do you want to praise God for? Write it down here: _____

_____

_____

_____

_____

SCRIPTURE READINGS - Read the scriptures first, then the writing. If you substitute your own scripture selections, make a note of them here:

> Proverbs 21
>
> John 10:15-18
>
> John 19:30

REFLECTIONS - If you were to write down one or two thoughts on what these scripture readings and the writing here means to you, they would be (write them down in the space provided): _____

_____

_____

_____

_____

_____

_____

REQUESTS - Write down what you want to request of God at this point in your journey. _____

_____

_____

_____

Thankful in Deliverance

I hate the evil, I hate the pain,
That we have run to again and again.
God deliver me, from this very hour.
Give me freedom, Give me freedom
Make me a part of Your kingdom
Spirit fill me with Your holy power.
Thank you Jesus, Thank you, Jesus,
For the battle You won for us.
You gave Your life in the battle freely.
Now we praise You, now we praise You.
You did not faint, from what You had to do.
With that one cross on the field, Calvary.

I hate the evil, I hate the pain,
That we have run to again and again.
God deliver us, from this very hour.
Give us freedom, Give us freedom
Make us a part of Your kingdom,
Spirit fill us, with Your holy power.
We praise You, Lord Jesus
You have stemmed the tide of evil's flood
We thank You, Lord Jesus
You have bought us life with Your blood
Jesus, You have made Your people free.

PRAYERS AND PRAISE - Go before the Father in Jesus' name. What are you thankful for? What do you want to praise God for? Write it down here: _____

_____

_____

_____

_____

SCRIPTURE READINGS - Read the scriptures first, then the writing. If you substitute your own scripture selections, make a note of them here:

> Proverbs 22
>
> Psalm 145:21
>
> Revelation 5:11-14

REFLECTIONS - If you were to write down one or two thoughts on what these scripture readings and the writing here means to you, they would be (write them down in the space provided): _____

_____

_____

_____

_____

_____

_____

REQUESTS - Write down what you want to request of God at this point in your journey. _____

_____

_____

_____

If I Never Stop Praising Your Name....

I love you, Jesus.
Jesus, I love you.
No mater how many times I say it,
Each and every time it's more true.

"Worthy" is not enough to describe
The praise and honor that You're due.
If I never stop praising Your name,
Jesus, I could never give too much honor to You.

I praise you, Jesus.
Jesus, I praise you.
No mater how many times I say it,
Each and every time it's more true.

"Worthy" is not enough to describe
The praise and honor that You're due.
If I never stop praising Your name,
Jesus, I could never give too much honor to You.

Prayers, Praise, and Reflections - Make additional notes here:

_____

_____

_____

_____

_____

_____

_____

_____

_____

_____

_____

_____

_____

_____

_____

_____

_____

_____

_____

_____

_____

_____

_____

_____

_____

I need you, Jesus.
Jesus, I need you.
No mater how many times I say it,
Each and every time it's more true.

"Worthy" is not enough to describe
The praise and honor that You're due.
If I never stop praising Your name,
Jesus, I could never give too much honor to You.

I serve you, Jesus.
Jesus, I serve you.
No mater how many times I say it,
Each and every time it's more true.

"Worthy" is not enough to describe
The praise and honor that You're due.
If I never stop praising Your name,
Jesus, I could never give too much honor to You.

I want you, Jesus.
Jesus, I want you.
No mater how many times I say it,
Each and every time it's more true.

Prayers, Praise, and Reflections - Make additional notes here:

_____

_____

_____

_____

_____

_____

_____

_____

_____

_____

_____

_____

_____

_____

_____

_____

_____

_____

_____

_____

_____

_____

_____

_____

_____

_____

"Worthy" is not enough to describe
The praise and honor that You're due.
If I never stop praising Your name,
Jesus, I could never give too much honor to You.

I long for you, Jesus.
Jesus, I long for you.
No mater how many times I say it,
Each and every time it's more true.

"Worthy" is not enough to. describe
The praise and honor that You're due.
If I never stop praising Your name,
Jesus, I could never give too much honor to You.

I live for you, Jesus.
Jesus, I live for you.
No mater how many times I say it,
Each and every time it's more true.

PRAYERS AND PRAISE - Go before the Father in Jesus' name. What are you thankful for? What do you want to praise God for? Write it down here: _____

_____

_____

_____

_____

SCRIPTURE READINGS - Read the scriptures first, then the writing. If you substitute your own scripture selections, make a note of them here:

      Proverbs 23   Mark 16:15-18

      Exodus 17:15

      Psalm 60:4

REFLECTIONS - If you were to write down one or two thoughts on what these scripture readings and the writing here means to you, they would be (write them down in the space provided): _____

_____

_____

_____

_____

_____

_____

REQUESTS - Write down what you want to request of God at this point in your journey. _____

_____

_____

_____

Let the Banner be Unfurled

Take my hand, oh God,
Lead me to prayer.
Take my hand, oh God,
I will meet You there.

I long to serve You, Jesus,
I want to show You to the world,
To the lost and dying,
To the sick, deaf, or crying,
Let the Banner be unfurled.
Take my hand, oh God
Lead me to prayer.
Take my hand, oh God,
I will meet You there.

I long to praise You, Jesus,
I want to give You to the world,
To the lost and dying,
To the sick, deaf, or crying,
Let the Banner be unfurled.
Take my life, oh God,
Lead me to prayer.
Take my life, oh God,
I will meet You there.

PRAYERS AND PRAISE - Go before the Father in Jesus' name. What are you thankful for? What do you want to praise God for? Write it down here: _____

_____

_____

_____

_____

SCRIPTURE READINGS - Read the scriptures first, then the writing. If you substitute your own scripture selections, make a note of them here:

Proverbs 24   I John 5:4

Hebrews 12:1-4

James 4:7-10

REFLECTIONS - If you were to write down one or two thoughts on what these scripture readings and the writing here means to you, they would be (write them down in the space provided): _____

_____

_____

_____

_____

_____

REQUESTS - Write down what you want to request of God at this point in your journey. _____

_____

_____

_____

Send Us Your Spirit

Making known to men the will of God,
Holy Spirit we receive You.
Use us to reach the lost and lonely,
Father, Your word is true.

We want to serve You, Lord
But, sometimes we stumble and fall.
You alone can help us,
We bow our knee to the All in All.

Making known to men the will of God,
Holy Spirit give us power.
The saints of God are Your messengers,
Spirit, come in this hour.

We want to be like You, Lord,
For no other had bled and died.
We want your strength in us,
With humbled hearts, surrendered pride.

Making known to men the will of God,
Holy Spirit come to us now.
Give us wisdom and power to serve,
Jesus, please show us how.

PRAYERS AND PRAISE - Go before the Father in Jesus' name. What are you thankful for? What do you want to praise God for? Write it down here: _____

_____

_____

_____

_____

SCRIPTURE READINGS - Read the scriptures first, then the writing. If you substitute your own scripture selections, make a note of them here:

> Proverbs 25   II Corinthians 5:17
>
> I Kings 17:21-24
>
> Ephesians 4:1-3

REFLECTIONS - If you were to write down one or two thoughts on what these scripture readings and the writing here means to you, they would be (write them down in the space provided): _____

_____

_____

_____

_____

_____

REQUESTS - Write down what you want to request of God at this point in your journey. _____

_____

_____

_____

Power over Death and Sin

The people

"Bend me or break me
Never forsake me.
Know my desire
Is to serve only You."

God

"If you believe in Me
Find yourself trusting Me.
Know My desire
Is living with you."

The people

"In my heart I purpose
To have a surplus,
Abundant desire
To give You my praise."

God

"You can believe it,
Trust and receive it,
Abundant desire,
Adds power to praise."

The people

"Help us be the ones who serve You
Give us power over death and sin.
Keep us mindful of the ransom,
The price You paid, Friend that You've been."

115

PRAYERS AND PRAISE - Go before the Father in Jesus' name. What are you thankful for? What do you want to praise God for? Write it down here: _____

_____

_____

_____

_____

SCRIPTURE READINGS - Read the scriptures first, then the writing. If you substitute your own scripture selections, make a note of them here:

> Proverbs 26   Ephesians 4:11-16
> Numbers 14:9,20
> Psalm 91:1-2

REFLECTIONS - If you were to write down one or two thoughts on what these scripture readings and the writing here means to you, they would be (write them down in the space provided): _____

_____

_____

_____

_____

_____

_____

REQUESTS - Write down what you want to request of God at this point in your journey. _____

_____

_____

_____

Comfort and Commandment

When at last you lay your head
Upon the pillow of stone,
Will the nation know whom you served?
Or will it be a secret, forever unknown?
Be not afraid, My child,
Be not afraid.
I have called you, I will keep you,
Be not afraid.

Stand and speak the words I give you,
Be not afraid.
I have called you, you know it's true,
Be not afraid.
Be not afraid, My child,
Be not afraid.
The gates of hell will not prevail against you,
Be not afraid.
Speak truth, like fire from a fountain,
Be not afraid.
Fire and smoke from God's Holy Mountain,
Be not afraid.

Be not afraid, My child
Be not afraid.

PRAYERS AND PRAISE - Go before the Father in Jesus' name. What are you thankful for? What do you want to praise God for? Write it down here: _____

_____

_____

_____

_____

SCRIPTURE READINGS - Read the scriptures first, then the writing. If you substitute your own scripture selections, make a note of them here:

     Proverbs 27   Revelation 15:3-4

     II Chronicles 20:14-23

     Jeremiah 33:10-11

REFLECTIONS - If you were to write down one or two thoughts on what these scripture readings and the writing here means to you, they would be (write them down in the space provided): _____

_____

_____

_____

_____

_____

_____

REQUESTS - Write down what you want to request of God at this point in your journey. _____

_____

_____

_____

Jesus is Forever Lord

The people

Each Time I'm tempted, Lord
May I only think of You.
Let Your Holy Spirit guide my thoughts,
My life, and my actions, too.

Jesus

"How many of you resisted unto death?
Felt the steel blade pierce your side.
The rushing thoughts with a last breath,
Or the parent's pain from another child who has lied?"

The people

Each time I'm tempted, Lord
May I only think of You.
Let Your Holy Spirit guide my thoughts,
My life, and my actions, too.

Jesus

"As you think on these things,
Know that I know each one well.
And I know the joy suffering brings,
When a saint is delivered from the grips of hell."

Prayers, Praise, and Reflections - Make additional notes here:

The people

And I will praise You, praise You,
Praise Your Name forevermore.
And You are Jesus, Jesus,
Jesus is forever Lord.

And We will praise You, praise You,
Praise Your Name forevermore.
And You are Jesus, Jesus,
Jesus is forever Lord.

PRAYERS AND PRAISE - Go before the Father in Jesus' name. What are you thankful for? What do you want to praise God for? Write it down here: _____

_____

_____

_____

_____

SCRIPTURE READINGS - Read the scriptures first, then the writing. If you substitute your own scripture selections, make a note of them here:

> **Proverbs 28**
> **Matthew 21:44**
> **Revelation 5:13**

REFLECTIONS - If you were to write down one or two thoughts on what these scripture readings and the writing here means to you, they would be (write them down in the space provided): _____

_____

_____

_____

_____

_____

_____

REQUESTS - Write down what you want to request of God at this point in your journey. _____

_____

_____

_____

(I Will) Break My Heart Upon Your Rock

[spoken]

Water's gentle lapping upon stone near a brook,
Pounding thunder of salty waves upon a beach,
The wonder in an infant's eye, laying in a cradle,
All of these are beyond my mind's reach.

[singing]

Lord, You have made them all,
Each one owes its praise to You,
For You alone can create or change,
Only Your words are forever true.

So I will praise You, though I be consumed,
For without You I am less than dust.
What good would it be to seek my life.
If in You I do not trust?

I will praise You till I am dust,
Knowing You only desire my good.
Please help me to remember
To only speak and do the things I should.

Prayers, Praise, and Reflections - Make additional notes here:

I will lift my hands to praise You,
Break my heart upon Your Rock.
May You show me Your desire,
Your mysteries please unlock.

Your miracles are above the heavens,
Your ways beyond those of man.
Though I alone cannot reach them,
By Your Spirit I know I can.

PRAYERS AND PRAISE - Go before the Father in Jesus' name. What are you thankful for? What do you want to praise God for? Write it down here: _____

_____

_____

_____

_____

_____

SCRIPTURE READINGS - Read the scriptures first, then the writing. If you substitute your own scripture selections, make a note of them here:

> Proverbs 29
>
> Revelation 4:8-11
>
> Revelation 5:8-10

REFLECTIONS - If you were to write down one or two thoughts on what these scripture readings and the writing here means to you, they would be (write them down in the space provided): _____

_____

_____

_____

_____

_____

_____

REQUESTS - Write down what you want to request of God at this point in your journey. _____

_____

_____

_____

A Wonder in Heaven

Ha-llelujah, Ha-llelujah!
Ha-llelujah, Ha-llelujah!
The pleasant odor of incense,
Do you hear the picture it paints?
Can you taste the fragrance,
Of the prayers of the saints?
"God is Worthy! God is Worthy!"
I hear all of creation groan,
"God is Holy! God is Holy!"
With words the kingdom is sewn.

Ha-llelujah, Ha-llelujah!
Ha-llelujah, Ha-llelujah!
Praise floats on wings around the throne.
The eagle, man, lion and calf,
Second the words heard from earth,
Singing power on our behalf.
"God is Worthy! God is Worthy!"
I hear all of creation groan,
"God is Holy! God is Holy!"
With words the kingdom is sewn.

Go for-rth!
Go for-rth!

PRAYERS AND PRAISE - Go before the Father in Jesus' name. What are you thankful for? What do you want to praise God for? Write it down here: _____

_____

_____

_____

_____

SCRIPTURE READINGS - Read the scriptures first, then the writing. If you substitute your own scripture selections, make a note of them here:

> Proverbs 30   Acts 3:4-9
>
> Leviticus 26:40-42
>
> John 3:16

REFLECTIONS - If you were to write down one or two thoughts on what these scripture readings and the writing here means to you, they would be (write them down in the space provided): _____

_____

_____

_____

_____

_____

_____

REQUESTS - Write down what you want to request of God at this point in your journey. _____

_____

_____

_____

Road to Inheritance

Loosen the bonds of the broken hearted,
Trample the walls of those that are bound,
Tear down the gates, the doors, and the bars,
Let repentance in your heart be found.

Troubles come and troubles go,
Some seem like they'll never end.
When your life seems too much to bear,
Closer than a brother is a Friend.

Loosen the bonds of the broken hearted,
Trample the walls of those that are bound,
Tear down the gates, the doors, and the bars,
Let redemption in your heart be found.

Life has ups and life has downs,
To the just and unjust God gives rain.
Wait upon the Lord for His blessing,
From the well doing do not refrain.

Loosen the bonds of the broken hearted,
Trample the walls of those that are bound,
Tear down the gates, the doors, and the bars,
Let restoration in your heart be found.

Prayers, Praise, and Reflections - Make additional notes here:

_____

_____

_____

_____

_____

_____

_____

_____

_____

_____

_____

_____

_____

_____

_____

_____

_____

_____

_____

_____

_____

_____

_____

_____

_____

_____

_____

Seek the Lord with your heart,
To Him give glory, honor, and praise.
Ask Him each day for His direction.
Praise to Jesus the Ancient of Days!

Loosen the bonds of the broken hearted,
Trample the walls of those that are bound,
Tear down the gates, the doors, and the bars,
Let revelation in your heart be found.

PRAYERS AND PRAISE - Go before the Father in Jesus' name. What are you thankful for? What do you want to praise God for? Write it down here: _____

_____

_____

_____

_____

SCRIPTURE READINGS - Read the scriptures first, then the writing. If you substitute your own scripture selections, make a note of them here:

> Proverbs 31
> John 14:12-14
> I Corinthians 14:12-15

REFLECTIONS - If you were to write down one or two thoughts on what these scripture readings and the writing here means to you, they would be (write them down in the space provided): _____

_____

_____

_____

_____

_____

REQUESTS - Write down what you want to request of God at this point in your journey. _____

_____

_____

The Song of _____'s Journey

(Fill in your name)

The heart of a child,
Precious and pure.
Lord, I receive it,
May Your righteousness endure.

I have come to thank You,
To glorify Your name.
I thank You for our journey,
May I never be the same.
For each and every of these moments
I will praise and magnify Your name.
Jesus, may I ever praise Your name.

(On these lines and the following pages. Takes one or two items from
each day and write them down, then praise the Lord for blessing you
on your journey!)

_____

_____

_____

_____

_____

_____

_____

_____

Prayers, Praise, and Reflections - Make additional notes here:

(Continue to write the summary of your journey.)

Prayers, Praise, and Reflections - Make additional notes here:

_____

_____

_____

_____

_____

_____

_____

_____

_____

_____

_____

_____

_____

_____

_____

_____

_____

_____

_____

_____

_____

_____

_____

_____

_____

_____

_____

(Continue to write the summary of your journey.)

Prayers, Praise, and Reflections - Make additional notes here:

_____

_____

_____

_____

_____

_____

_____

_____

_____

_____

_____

_____

_____

_____

_____

_____

_____

_____

_____

_____

_____

_____

_____

(Continue to write the summary of your journey.)

_____

_____

_____

_____

_____

_____

_____

_____

_____

_____

_____

_____

_____

_____

_____

_____

_____

_____

_____

_____

_____

_____

Epilogue

Epilogue

Well, how was it? I hope your journey (if that is how you used this book) was as beneficial for you as it was for me. God in His holiness is so worthy to be praised! How great a freedom there is in serving Him with your whole heart!

I wanted to thank you once again for allowing me to share this work with you. I trust that the habits you have now developed will be a treasure to you. Praying. Reading God's holy bible. Praising His name. Calling out to Him in times of trial and temptation. He alone can deliver us. He is faithful and just, and we can depend on Him to deliver us when we call out to Him in Jesus' name! Hallelujah!!

Now, go into the land and do the works of Jesus, beginning at home. God bless you!